W9-BVP-689

EDGE BOOKS™

• WAR VEHICLES •

# VEHICLES of WORLD WAR II

by Eric Fein

Consultant:
Dennis P. Mroczkowski
Colonel, U.S. Marine Corps Reserve (Retired)
Williamsburg, Virginia

CAPSTONE PRESS
a capstone imprint

Edge Books are published by Capstone Press,
1710 Roe Crest Drive, North Mankato, Minnesota 56003
www.capstonepub.com

**Library of Congress Cataloging-in-Publication Data**
Fein, Eric.
Vehicles of World War II / by Eric Fein.
pages cm.—(Edge books. War vehicles)
Includes bibliographical references and index.
Summary: "Describes various land, air, and sea vehicles used by the Axis Powers and
the Allied Powers during World War II"—Provided by publisher.
Audience: Ages 8–14.
ISBN 978-1-4296-9915-0 (library binding)
ISBN 978-1-4765-3380-3 (eBook PDF)
1. Vehicles, Military—History—20th century—Juvenile literature. 2. World War,
1939–1945—Transportation—Juvenile literature. 3. World War, 1939–1945—Equipment
and supplies—Juvenile literature. I. Title.
UG615.F45 2014
940.54—dc23                                                          2013005608

**Editorial Credits**
Aaron Sautter, editor; Heidi Thompson, designer; Eric Manske, production specialist

Printed in the United States of America in Stevens Point, Wisconsin.
052014  008277R

# Table of Contents

# Ch.1 The World Fights Back

It was the dead of night. Thousands of **Allied forces** warships steamed across the English Channel near France. More than 1,000 C-47 cargo planes carried thousands of **paratroopers** to be dropped behind enemy lines.

In the early dawn of June 6, 1944, the Allies launched one of the biggest and bloodiest battles in history. The D-Day landings at Normandy, France, were a turning point in World War II (1939–1945). But the Allies' efforts wouldn't have succeeded without the thousands of military vehicles used in the invasion.

## WAR FACT

The nations at war were divided into the Allied forces, or Allies, and the Axis powers. The Allies included Britain, the United States, France, the Soviet Union, China, and Canada. The Axis countries included Germany, Italy, and Japan.

**Allied forces**—countries united against Germany during World War II, including France, the United States, Great Britain, and the Soviet Union

**paratrooper**—a soldier trained to jump by parachute into battle

After losing World War I (1914–1918), Germany was forced to pay for the damage it had caused. This left the country poor. The German people wanted their country to be a strong and respected nation. In the 1930s German leader Adolph Hitler and the Nazi party promised to restore Germany to greatness. Once in power, Hitler soon began taking over other countries in Europe.

More than 5,000 ships and 13,000 aircraft were used in the D-Day landings.

At about the same time, Japan was taking over parts of Asia and several Pacific islands. Great Britain, the United States, the Soviet Union, and other countries joined together to stop Germany and Japan. The war soon became the biggest and bloodiest conflict the world had ever seen.

## IMPROVED TECHNOLOGY

Combat vehicles like airplanes, submarines, and tanks were used for the first time in World War I. But by World War II, military vehicles were greatly improved. Advancements like accurate bombsights made airplanes deadlier in combat. **Radar** was especially useful for finding and tracking enemy aircraft. Navy ships used **sonar** to help crewmembers learn the distance and depth of enemy submarines.

By World War II, tanks had become primary land combat vehicles. They were designed and built to have a good balance of speed, firepower, and protective armor. They also carried radios to help troops organize attacks on the battlefield.

**radar**—a device that uses radio waves to track the location of objects

**sonar**—a device that uses sound waves to find underwater objects

Both Allied and Axis forces used radar to find and track enemy aircraft.

The advancements made during the war would forever change the way wars were fought. Military vehicles were stronger, faster, and more powerful than ever. Since World War II, military forces have relied on powerful vehicles of war to find victory on the battlefield.

## ···ALLIED TANKS···

During the war Allied forces used many land vehicles, including armored cars and troop transports. Powerful tanks played a major role in combat. Some tanks were modified for special uses such as clearing mines or shooting flames.

## M4 Sherman Tank

The Sherman was the standard battle tank for the U.S. Army. It was used in combat in North Africa, Italy, France, and Germany. The Sherman's main gun fired 75-millimeter wide shells. Shermans were also armed with three heavy machine guns. Shermans were operated by a five-man crew. About 50,000 Sherman tanks were built during the war.

## WAR FACT

Shermans at the D-Day invasion of Normandy were specially modified with water seals, canvas rubber walls, and two propellers in the rear. These duplex-drive tanks could travel both through water and on land. But many of them sank before they could get to the beach.

# Russian T-34

Soviet T-34 tanks were well armored and well armed. They were used in small, fast-moving groups to attack Axis positions. The T-34's tracks were almost 2 feet (0.6 meter) wide, which helped it move easily through deep mud and snow.

# Churchill Tank

The British Churchill tank saw its first action at Dieppe, France, in 1942. The Churchill was smaller than many other tanks. Its size made it a difficult target for enemy tanks. The Churchill moved well over all types of terrain. The British built several versions of the Churchill tank. Some were used as **flamethrowers**.

# Matilda Tank

The British Matilda was used in early battles in France in 1940. It was also used in North Africa against German forces. The tank's front armor was 3 inches (7.6 centimeters) thick, making it hard to stop. But Germany soon began using powerful 88 mm guns against Allied tanks. The heavy shells could punch through even the Matildas' thick armor.

**flamethrower**—a weapon that shoots a stream of burning liquid

## Ha-Go Tank

This small Japanese tank was not heavily armored, making it fast and easy to drive. However, it was cramped and uncomfortable inside. The Ha-Go was used mostly in China, Burma, and on Pacific islands until 1943.

## Tiger I Tank

At 60 tons (54 metric tons), the German Tiger tank was one of the largest tanks of the war. Its armor was so thick that 75 mm shells couldn't damage it. The Tiger's 88 mm main gun was one of the largest tank guns in the war. The best way to stop a Tiger was to damage its treads. But later in the war, the Allies had success against the Tiger using heavier guns.

# Panther Tank

German Panther tanks fired armor-piercing shells. Panthers were used in Europe and eastern Russia. They did well against Shermans, Churchills, and T-34s. The Panther's angled front armor and wide tracks were similar to those of the Soviet T-34 tank.

# Tiger Elefant

Germany used a design similar to the Tiger tank for the Tiger Elefant. These tank destroyers were first used in combat in July 1943. But they often had mechanical problems. They broke down, got stuck, and were sometimes captured by enemy forces.

# The Maus

*Maus* is German for "mouse." But there was nothing small about this German tank. The Maus was the heaviest tank ever built. Only two were made, but neither saw combat. Allied forces captured one and destroyed the other near the end of the war. The tanks weighed more than 180 tons (163 metric tons) and were more than 30 feet (9 m) long.

## Churchill Ark

The British Churchill Ark was a mobile ramp made from the body of a Churchill tank. Its ramps were about 12 feet (3.7 m) long on the front and back. It could create a bridge across a 30-foot (9-m) ditch.

## DUKW "Duck"

The DUKW was an **amphibious** U.S. vehicle that was shaped like a boat and had six wheels. It could carry 25 fully-equipped soldiers or up to 5,000 pounds (2,300 kg) of cargo. It was first used during the invasion of Sicily in July 1943.

## WAR FACT

The letters DUKW stood for:
D=model year 1942
U=utility
K=all-wheel drive
W=dual rear axles

**amphibious**—a vehicle or craft that can travel over land or in water

# Half-Track

U.S.-built half-tracks came in various models. The M3 could seat 13 soldiers. Some half-tracks had mounted machine guns and a winch or an obstacle roller. Soldiers used winches to help pull other vehicles out of deep mud. Rollers helped keep half-tracks from getting stuck when driving over large objects.

## Horses and Other Animals

Both the Allies and Axis forces used animals to transport men and supplies. In some cases, horses and donkeys were used to travel to locations that trucks and tanks couldn't. During Germany's invasion of the Soviet Union in 1941, 700,000 horses were used to pull supply wagons and artillery. In places such as China, Burma, and India, camels and elephants were used to carry supplies. The United States used dogs to pull sleds in Alaska and Greenland. The Germans used dogs and reindeer to pull supply sleds.

**artillery**—cannons and other large guns used during battles

## ···ALLIED BATTLESHIPS AND AIRCRAFT CARRIERS···

World War II brought major advancements to naval warfare. Battleships became bigger and more powerful than ever before. Aircraft carriers could launch planes directly into war zones. And submarines became important for their ability to launch surprise attacks against enemy ships.

## HMS *Warspite*

In March 1941 the British battleship HMS *Warspite* helped destroy Italy's naval forces in the Mediterranean Sea. The battleship later provided support during the D-Day invasion at Normandy. Along with its eight 15-inch (38-centimeter) main guns, *Warspite* also carried 18 smaller guns and four **torpedo** tubes.

**torpedo**—an underwater missile used to blow up a target

# USS *Iowa*

The USS *Iowa* was launched on August 27, 1942. At the time, the *Iowa* class battleships were the fastest ever built. Their nine 16-inch (40.6-cm) guns were also the largest ever mounted on U.S. battleships. The *Iowa* also carried 20 5-inch (12.7-cm) guns and a total of 129 anti-aircraft guns. The *Iowa* was used in many major naval battles in the Pacific Ocean during the war.

# USS *Lexington*

The USS *Lexington* was originally designed as a quicker kind of battleship called a battle cruiser. But in 1922 an aircraft hangar and flight deck were added to turn the ship into an aircraft carrier. The *Lexington* was also armed with eight 8-inch (20-cm) guns and 12 anti-aircraft guns. It could carry more than 90 aircraft. On May 8, 1942, Japanese planes attacked the *Lexington* in the Coral Sea near the Solomon Islands. The ship was damaged beyond repair. The U.S. Navy sank it to prevent the Japanese from capturing it.

# Bismarck

Germany's battleship *Bismarck* staged hit and run attacks in the Atlantic Ocean and the North Sea. The ship was armed with a huge number of deadly guns. It carried eight large 380 mm main guns and 74 smaller guns. It could also carry up to four airplanes. In May 1941 British warships battled the *Bismarck* near Bergen, Norway. The *Bismarck* took heavy damage and was sunk by the HMS *Dorsetshire*.

# Yamato

The Japanese battleship *Yamato* had even more firepower than Germany's *Bismarck*. It was armed with nine 18-inch (46-cm) guns, six 6-inch (15-cm) guns, and 190 smaller guns. It could also carry up to seven aircraft. On April 7, 1945, the *Yamato* was sent on a difficult mission to take back Okinawa island from the Allies. But Allied forces learned of Japan's plans and sank the *Yamato* before it could complete its mission.

# Akagi

The Japanese aircraft carrier *Akagi* led the attack on Pearl Harbor, Hawaii, on December 7, 1941. *Akagi* took part in several sea battles and sank many ships. It was armed with six 8-inch (20-cm) guns, twelve 4.7-inch (12-cm) guns, and 28 anti-aircraft guns. It could carry up to 91 aircraft. U.S. naval ships and planes destroyed the *Akagi* during the Battle of Midway in 1942.

## Warships in Disguise

To get close to Allied ships, the Axis used a trick that pirates often used in the 1700s. Some of their warships flew non-Axis flags to appear as friendly merchant ships. When an Allied ship got close enough, the disguised Axis ship would open fire. Germany had nine such ships, Italy had three, and Japan had two. Together these ships sank 110 Allied ships and captured 31.

# Admiral Graf Spee

The *Admiral Graf Spee* was a German pocket battleship. It was smaller than a regular battleship, but it had similar weapons and armor. The *Admiral Graf Spee* was used to raid ships in the Atlantic.

# HMS *Turbulent*

This British Triton class submarine had 11 torpedo tubes. The Allies used the HMS *Turbulent* for several daring attacks. It once attacked German land forces in Libya. This was a risky move. By surfacing to use the deck gun, the submarine became a target for German artillery. In 1942 *Turbulent* attacked an Italian **convoy** and sank every ship in it.

# Japanese I-400 Class Submarines

At the time, the Japanese I-400 class submarines were the largest in the world. They were 400 feet (122 m) long and could carry and launch three small bomber planes. Three I-400s were completed near the end of the war, but they never entered combat. The Allies seized them when Japan surrendered.

**convoy**—a group of vehicles traveling together

# USS *Archer-Fish*

The USS *Archer-Fish* made the biggest kill in the history of submarine warfare. The U.S. sub sank the *Shinano*, a Japanese aircraft carrier, on November 29, 1944. The *Shinano* had just entered the war 10 days earlier. The *Archer-Fish* was equipped with 10 torpedo tubes, one 4-inch (10-cm) deck gun, and two small cannons.

## WAR FACT

On October 24, 1944, the U.S. sub USS *Tang* attacked a Japanese convoy and escaped unharmed. The next night the *Tang* attacked another convoy. In just 24 hours the *Tang* sank eight enemy ships.

# German U-boats

Germany's "undersea boats," or U-boats, caused many problems for the Allies during the war. They often attacked and sank Allied supply ships. U-boats were armed with five torpedo tubes and one or two large deck guns. On September 17, 1939, *U-29* became the first German sub to sink an Allied warship. It hit the British aircraft carrier HMS *Courageous* with three torpedoes.

## PT Boats

Patrol Torpedo (PT) boats were small plywood vessels armed with two or four torpedo tubes. They also carried a cannon and machine guns. PT boats could travel up to 31 miles (50 km) per hour on the water. Because of their speed and small size, enemy ships had difficulty spotting and targeting PT boats. They were mainly used in the Mediterranean Sea and among the islands in the Pacific.

## WAR FACT

On August 2, 1943, PT 109 was destroyed by a Japanese warship. The boat's captain led the survivors to a tiny island. He then swam to another island to find help. The crew was rescued several days later. The captain's heroics made PT 109 famous. The captain, John F. Kennedy, later became the U.S. president in 1960.

## Higgins Boats

Higgins boats were designed to deliver soldiers from ships to the shore. The boats had flat bottoms and hinged front ends to easily release soldiers onto the beach. Higgins boats played a critical role in the D-Day landings at Normandy.

# Landing Craft, Infantry (LCI)

U.S.-built LCIs were 160 feet (49 m) long and carried close to 200 soldiers. These boats had ramps on both sides of their bows to give soldiers fast and easy access to landing sites. LCIs were used in many major battles, including D-Day.

# Midget Submarines

British midget submarines, or X-crafts, were 48 feet (14.6 m) long. They carried a crew of four. They were used for sneak attacks against large Axis ships. These small subs were also used for scouting the beaches at Normandy before the D-Day landings.

# Landing Ship Tank (LST)

U.S. LSTs were 327 feet (99.7 m) long and had flat bottoms, which made them slow. U.S. soldiers joked that LST stood for "Long, Slow Target." But the LST's design allowed it to run right up onto a beach. When LSTs landed, their bow doors opened to allow tanks and other land vehicles to drive directly onto the shore.

## •••ALLIED FIGHTERS AND BOMBERS•••

Airplanes became a major military vehicle for the first time in World War II. Huge bombers could carry and drop thousands of pounds of bombs on enemy positions. Fighter planes armed with machine guns and cannons controlled the skies.

## P-51D Mustang

The U.S.-built Mustang was a long-range **escort** and ground attack fighter. The Mustang is known for destroying more enemy aircraft than any other U.S. fighter in Europe.

## Mitchell B-25

The U.S.-built Mitchell B-25H was one of the most heavily armed planes ever made. It was equipped with a 75 mm cannon, 14 machine guns, and carried 3,000 pounds (1,360 kilograms) of bombs. In total, B-25s flew more than 60,000 missions and dropped more than 80,000 tons (72,600 metric tons) of bombs.

**escort**—to travel with and protect

# Supermarine Spitfire

The British Spitfire was used as a fighter-bomber and **reconnaissance** plane. Its long wingspan and rounded wingtips helped increase its speed. The Spitfire went through 40 major changes during the war. The MKIIA was equipped with eight machine guns. The MKIV was designed for spying. It carried two cameras and an extra fuel tank.

# B-29 Superfortress

The U.S. B-29 Superfortress was a long-range heavy bomber. It gave the United States a strong advantage in fighting the war in the Pacific Ocean. Using Pacific islands as bases, the B-29 could bring the fight to Japan. Each plane could carry about 20,000 pounds (9,100 kg) of bombs.

**reconnaissance**—a mission to gather information about an enemy

## Junker JU 87

When the German Junker dove toward a target, it made a noise that sounded like a scream or a shriek. This bomber had early success in Poland and France. However, Junkers had little success during the Battle of Britain in 1940. The planes were no match for Britain's faster, more nimble fighters.

## Mitsubishi G4M (Betty)

This bomber was widely used by the Imperial Japanese Navy. It had a range of more than 2,200 miles (3,540 km) and could carry more than 2,200 pounds (1,000 kg) of bombs or torpedoes. Japanese pilots nicknamed it the flying cigar. It tended to catch fire because of poorly designed fuel tanks.

# Focke Wulf Fw 190 A-8

German Focke Wulf fighter planes were armed with machine guns, cannons, and bombs. The Focke Wulf Fw was first used in combat in the summer of 1941. Britain captured one of these fighters in June 1942. After studying it, they created the Hawker Fury, which used many of the Focke Wulf's features.

# Mitsubishi A6M Reisen (Zero)

The Japanese A6M Reisen, often called the Zero fighter by Allied pilots, was a ship-based plane. These fighters were used in the attack on Pearl Harbor and most major battles in the Pacific. Zeroes were often used in **kamikaze** attacks against Allied ships.

**kamikaze**—a Japanese pilot who would purposely crash his plane into a target, resulting in his own death

# Supermarine Walrus

The British Supermarine Walrus was an amphibious utility plane. It was used for reconnaissance missions and air and sea rescues. Instead of wheels, it had pontoons, or floats, to land on the water. The Walrus was the first seaplane to be launched by a warship.

# Consolidated PBY Catalina

U.S.-built Catalinas were workhorses during the war. These utility planes were used as bombers, convoy escorts, air and sea rescue planes, and transport planes. They were also used to pull **gliders**. Specialized Catalinas were used to attack Japanese ships at night. These planes were painted black and nicknamed Black Cats.

**glider**—a lightweight aircraft that flies by floating on air currents instead of using engines

# Waco CG-4A Glider

The U.S. Waco Glider could carry 15 people, including the pilot and co-pilot. These planes were often used to quietly carry troops behind enemy lines. They proved valuable during the invasions of Sicily in 1943 and Normandy in 1944. The Waco Glider was usually towed by a C-46 or C-47 cargo plane. Its large wingspan stretched 84 feet (26 m). Its lightweight body was built with plywood, canvas, and steel tubes.

## WAR FACT

Gliders were first used in World War II on May 10, 1940. Germany used them in a major air campaign over Western Europe.

# Messerschmitt ME 321

The German Messerschmitt was about four times larger than any British or U.S. glider. The ME 321 was able to transport 24 tons (22 metric tons) of cargo, or 200 fully-equipped soldiers.

Throughout the war, both sides invented new and sometimes unusual vehicles. Many were built and used in total secrecy. Others were used openly. Some were successful, but others never achieved the inventors' original goals.

## Remote-Controlled Tanks

These armored unmanned vehicles were operated with radio signals from as far as 1 mile (1.6 km) away. Some of these tanks were loaded with explosives and used as remote-controlled bombs.

## Focke-Ahgelis FA-330 Bachstelze

The Bachstelze rotor kite was shaped similarly to a helicopter. It was pulled from a line attached to the rear of a U-boat. It flew up to 400 feet (122 m) in the air. An observer sat in the craft to watch for enemy ships. When a ship was spotted, the aircraft was pulled down with a winch before the submarine submerged. The Allies didn't learn about these machines until the end of the war.

# Messerschmitt ME 163 Komet

Germany began using the ME 163 Komet in 1944. It was the first successful rocket-propelled combat aircraft. It was armed with two 30 mm cannons and could reach speeds of more than 600 miles (966 km) per hour. This speed was almost twice as fast as standard fighter planes of the time.

## Gloster Meteor

The British-built Gloster Meteor was the only Allied jet-powered fighter plane to see combat during the war. These planes entered the fighting in 1944 against Germany's V1 flying bombs. The Meteor could reach speeds of more than 400 miles (644 km) per hour.

# Glossary

**Allied forces** (AL-eyed FORSS-uhs)—countries united against Germany during World War II, including France, the United States, Great Britain, and Soviet Union

**amphibious** (am-FI-bee-uhs)—a vehicle or craft that can travel over land or in water

**artillery** (ar-TIL-uh-ree)—cannons and other large guns used during battles

**convoy** (kahn-VOY)—a group of vehicles traveling together

**escort** (es-KORT)—to travel with and protect

**flamethrower** (FLAYM-throh-uhr)—a weapon that shoots a stream of burning liquid

**glider** (GLYE-dur)—a lightweight aircraft that flies by floating on air currents instead of using engines

**kamikaze** (kah-mi-KAH-zee)—a Japanese pilot during World War II who would purposely crash his plane into a target, resulting in his own death

**paratrooper** (PAIR-uh-troop-ur)—a soldier trained to jump by parachute into battle

**radar** (RAY-dar)—a device that uses radio waves to track the location of objects

**reconnaissance** (ree-KAH-nuh-suhnss)—a mission to gather information about an enemy

**sonar** (SOH-nar)—a device that uses sound waves to find underwater objects; sonar stands for sound navigation and ranging

**torpedo** (tor-PEE-doh)—an underwater missile used to blow up a target

# Read More

**Burgan, Michael.** *Weapons, Gear, and Uniforms of World War II.* Equipped for Battle. Mankato, Minn.: Capstone Press, 2012.

**Chrisp, Peter.** *World War II: Fighting for Freedom, 1939–1945.* New York: Scholastic, 2010.

**Perritano, John.** *World War II.* America At War. New York: Franklin Watts, 2010.

# Internet Sites

FactHound offers a safe, fun way to find Internet sites related to this book. All of the sites on FactHound have been researched by our staff.

Here's all you do:

Visit *www.facthound.com*

Type in this code: 9781429699150

Super-cool stuff!
Check out projects, games and lots more at
**www.capstonekids.com**

# Index